THE LOW CALORIE COOKBOOK

Julia Roles

OCTOPUS

Weights and Measures

All measurements in this book are based on Imperial weights and measures, with American equivalents given in parentheses. Measurements in weight in the Imperial and American system are the same. Measurements in volume are different, and each recipe gives the equivalents. Level spoon measures are used in all the recipes, unless otherwise specified.

Liquid measurements

1 Imperial pint	20 fluid ounces
1 American pint	16 fluid ounces
1 American cup	8 fluid ounces

Metric measures for easy reference

1 oz.	25 g.
8 oz.	225 g.
1 lb.	450 g.
5 fl. oz.	150 ml.
10 fl. oz.	300 ml.
1 Imperial pint	600 ml.
$\frac{1}{4}$ teaspoon	1×1.25 ml. spoon
$\frac{1}{2}$ teaspoon	1×2.5 ml. spoon
1 teaspoon	1×5 ml. spoon
1 tablespoon	1×15 ml. spoon

First published 1977 by
Octopus Books Limited
59 Grosvenor Street,
London W1

© 1977 Octopus Books Limited

ISBN 0 7064 0637 0

Produced by Mandarin Publishers Limited
22a Westlands Road,
Quarry Bay, Hong Kong

Printed in Hong Kong

CONTENTS

Weights and measures	6
Introduction	8
Soups and appetizers	16
Vegetables and salads	30
Fish	38
Meat and poultry	42
Table-top cookery	64
Desserts	74
Drinks, sauces and extras	83
Index	92

Frontispiece: DEVILLED CHICKEN (*Photograph by Tabasco Pepper Sauce*)

Introduction

The successful diet is one that lasts. And the reason it lasts is that it is interesting – so interesting in fact that it becomes a regular eating pattern. A diet doesn't have to be gimmicky in order to succeed. There is no need to exist on half a grapefruit and a hard-boiled egg each day. The secret to successful slimming is to follow a diet that is healthy, simple and, above all, varied. The most effortless way of doing this is to count calories. A calorie-counted diet is interesting, easy to calculate and maintain, and enables you to eat most of the foods you enjoy. The Low Calorie Cookbook takes slimming one stage further. Having explained the 'whys and wherefores' of following a diet, it gives a wealth of recipes for a wide variety of dishes, each one with its own calorie count.

Counting calories

Fat is no longer thought of as something which makes one healthy, contented and wise. People who are overweight are more prone to accidents, illness and shortness of breath, and often to depression. It is amazing just how many thin people are trying to get out of a fat shell, but lack the willpower or knowledge. A calorie-counted diet can work for everybody, irrespective of whether you want to shed a few pounds or get rid of an excess two stone.

A calorie is the name given to a small measure of heat. When food is digested, the body converts it into fuel, which is then burnt up to create energy. In order to maintain a constant weight your energy input (food) has to be balanced by your energy output (exercise and activity). The energy from food is counted in calories, and in order to lose weight you have to expend more calories per day in exercise than the calories you consume in your daily diet.

How many calories?

Your calorie intake depends on your way of life and the type of person you are. Some people have daily energy needs of more than 4000 calories, whereas others can exist quite happily on less than 2000. Fat people are not necessarily gluttons, and they do not necessarily eat more than thin people. Their only fault is that they are eating, or at some time have eaten, more food than their body needs.

The first thing you have to do is decide upon your energy gap. This

SOMERSET PORK (*Photograph by Taunton Cider*)

means that you have to calculate your output of calories, so that you can then work out how many calories you can afford to take in, in the form of food. Men, on the whole, use up more calories in the expenditure of energy during a day than women do. A man doing a sedentary office job uses up approximately 2600 calories to maintain a constant weight; a woman doing a similar job uses up only 1800–2000. In order to lose weight, the man needs to reduce his daily intake of calories to 2000 or less, and the woman needs to reduce hers to between 1000 and 1200.

What is your best weight?

There are no hard and fast rules about the relationship between the weight of a human body and its height and general structure. The following charts, however, provide a useful guide. Their main purpose is to help you calculate whether you are actually overweight, or whether you would just prefer to be slimmer. In each case, the weights are for men and women of medium frame, without clothes:

MEN		WOMEN	
HEIGHT	WEIGHT	HEIGHT	WEIGHT
ft. ins.	st. lbs.	ft. ins.	st. lbs.
5 0	8 11 (123 lbs.)	4 8	7 11 (109 lbs.)
5 1	8 13 (125 lbs.)	4 9	7 13 (111 lbs.)
5 2	9 1 (127 lbs.)	4 10	8 1 (113 lbs.)
5 3	9 4 (130 lbs.)	4 11	8 3 (115 lbs.)
5 4	9 7 (133 lbs.)	5 0	8 5 (117 lbs.)
5 5	9 11 (137 lbs.)	5 1	8 7 (119 lbs.)
5 6	10 1 (141 lbs.)	5 2	8 9 (121 lbs.)
5 7	10 5 (145 lbs.)	5 3	8 12 (124 lbs.)
5 8	10 9 (149 lbs.)	5 4	9 2 (128 lbs.)
5 9	10 13 (153 lbs.)	5 5	9 5 (131 lbs.)
5 10	11 4 (158 lbs.)	5 6	9 9 (135 lbs.)
5 11	11 9 (163 lbs.)	5 7	9 13 (139 lbs.)
6 0	12 1 (169 lbs.)	5 8	10 3 (143 lbs.)
6 1	12 7 (175 lbs.)	5 9	10 7 (147 lbs.)
6 2	12 13 (181 lbs.)	5 10	10 11 (151 lbs.)
6 3	13 5 (187 lbs.)	5 11	11 0 (154 lbs.)
6 4	13 11 (193 lbs.)	6 0	11 4 (158 lbs.)

Remember that it is important to weigh yourself first thing in the morning, as soon as you get up. Your body weight is at its most stable at this time, and you are not weighing food consumed during that day.

Tips for successful slimming

* Find a photograph of yourself at an ideal weight, to spur you on
* Hunt out a garment that you once wore, and would like to get into again
* Take a long look at yourself without clothes in a mirror, *sideways*
* Try to persuade someone else to slim at the same time – it greatly helps willpower
* If you have to go out to dinner, cut down on your amount of calories for the few days before, so that you have some spare calories in hand
* Keep tempting foods, such as sweets, out of reach
* Keep a calorie chart with you at all times
* Draw up a graph of your weight loss, to see how you progress
* Add variety to your meals so that they do not become boring
* Don't weigh yourself *too* frequently – ideally every third day
* Be as active as possible, walking rather than taking a bus whenever possible
* *Most important of all*, keep a record of your daily calorie intake

Using your Low Calorie Cookbook

A calorie chart is provided giving the calorific value of all the most popular everyday foods, to help you calculate your daily calorie intake. A calorie count per portion is given for each of the recipes, and the following pointers will help you to use the recipes to their best effect:

* Don't be tempted to increase any of the ingredient quantities, otherwise you will unbalance the calorie count
* Always use reconstituted skimmed milk powder in place of cows' milk
* Grill rather than fry whenever possible – food can be cooked in a non-stick pan without using fat
* Use a cheese that is comparatively low in calories, compared with other cheeses – Edam and Gouda are both good choices
* If a recipe includes a small amount of cream, it has been calculated in the calorific value – this can be further reduced by substituting natural yogurt
* Remove as much visible fat as you can from meat before cooking
* Have a pair of accurate scales for weighing ingredients
* Many of the recipes can be adapted to use other ingredients, e.g. using veal in place of pork. Check the appropriate calorie counts on the chart so that you can calculate the total calorie count of the recipe.

Calorie chart

In each case, the number of calories quoted is per oz. (28 g.) of food, unless otherwise stated. All foods are calorie counted on the raw weight, unless weight, unless otherwise stated.

DAIRY PRODUCE AND FATS

Beef dripping	262
Butter	226
Cheese	
Camembert	88
Cheddar	120
Cream	232
Danish Blue	103
Dutch	88
Gorgonzola	112
Parmesan	118
Cream	
single	62
double	131
soured	57
Eggs	46
Instant dessert topping reconstituted	34
Lard	262
Margarine	226
low fat spread	105
Milk	
full fat	19
skimmed	10
evaporated	45
condensed	100
Oil	260
Suet	262
Yogurt	
natural fat-free	15
sweetened fruit	32

CEREALS, CAKES AND BISCUITS

Arrowroot	101
Biscuits	
digestive	140
water	127
Branded breakfast cereals	100–104
Breads	
white or brown	70
malt	68

Ryvita	98
Vitawheat	120
Cakes	
chocolate	141
gingerbread	108
plain fruit	107
sponge	87
Cornflour	100
Custard powder	100
Flour	100
Macaroni	102
Malted breakfast cereal	88
Noodles	102
Oatmeal	115
Pearl barley	102
Rice	102
Semolina	100
Spaghetti	104

VEGETABLES

Aubergine	4
Beans	
baked	26
broad	12
butter	25
French or runner	5
Beetroot, boiled	12
Brussels sprouts	9
Cabbage	7
Carrots	6
Cauliflower	7
Celery	3
Chicory	3
Corn on the cob (1 cob)	84
Courgettes	4
Cucumber	3
Leeks	9
Lettuce	3
Marrow	4
Mushrooms	2
Onions	7

(continued on page 14)

VEAL ESCALOPES WITH LEMON (*Photograph by Jif Lemon Bureau*)

Parsnips	14	Shrimps, shelled	32
Peas	20	Sole	24
Green pepper	9	Trout	29
Potatoes, unpeeled	25	Tuna, canned	72
Tomatoes	4	Turbot	28
Watercress	4		

FRUIT AND NUTS

Almonds, shelled	170		
Apple	13		
Apricots			
fresh	8		
dried	50		
Avocado pear	25		
Banana	22		
Blackberries	8		
Blackcurrants	8		
Cherries, with stones	11		
Dates, stoned	70		
Dried fruit (currants, raisins, etc.)	70		
Gooseberries	5		
Grapefruit	3		
Grapes	17		
Melon (flesh only)	7		
Peaches	9		
Pears	11		
Pineapple	13		
Plums, with stones	10		
Prunes, with stones	38		
Raspberries	7		
Rhubarb	2		
Strawberries	7		
Walnuts, shelled	156		

MEAT, POULTRY AND GAME

Bacon	
back	115
streaky	150
Beef	
grilling steak	50
stewing steak	77
topside	60
Beefburger (1 frozen)	160
Chicken, boned	33
Duck, roasted	89
Ham, lean only	62
Kidney	28
Lamb, lean without bone	76
Liver	41
Luncheon meat	95
Pheasant, roast without bone	38
Pork, lean without bone	80
Rabbit, with bone	30
Sausage	
1 beef	190
1 pork	216
Tongue	87
Turkey, roast without bone	56
Veal	31
Venison, roast without bone	56

FISH

Cod	20
Cockles	14
Crab (flesh only)	36
Fish cakes (1 cake)	85
Fish fingers (1 finger)	50
Haddock	
fresh	20
smoked	18
Halibut	40
Herring	40
Kipper	38
Lobster, with shell	12
Mackerel	29
Mussels, with shells	0·75
Pilchards	54
Plaice	22
Prawns, peeled	30
Salmon	
fresh	46
canned	39
Sardines	80

PUDDINGS, PRESERVES AND SWEETS

Apple crumble	63
Apple pie	54
Blancmange, plain	34
Bread and butter pudding	46
Butterscotch	116
Chocolate	
milk	167
plain	155
Chocolate caramel bar (1 whole)	250
Chutney, tomato	43
Custard	33
Custard tart	82
Fruit salad, canned	20
Honey	82
Jam	75
Jelly (made-up packet)	23
Lemon curd	86
Marmalade	74
Mincemeat	37
Mince pies (1 pie)	120
Potato crisps	159
Salad cream	111

Steamed sponge pudding	104	Coffee	
Sugar	112	black no sugar	0
Trifle	43	with milk and sugar	16
		Fruit squashes and cordials	38
		Gin	63
BEVERAGES		Juices	
		natural orange	15
Beer		tomato	7
brown ale	8	Sherry	
Guinness	21	dry	33
Blackcurrant cordial	65	sweet	38
Brandy	63	Tea	
Cider		black no sugar	0
dry	10	with milk and sugar	10
sweet	12	Whisky	63
Cocoa		Wine	
made with milk and no sugar	28	dry	18
Cola-type drinks	14	sweet	25

Slimmers footnote
Always consult your doctor before embarking on any sort of diet. Most people can follow a diet quite safely, but it is advisable to get medical approval.

Where alternative ingredients are given, for example veal or pork, the calorie count refers to the ingredient with the lower calorie value.

Where the recipe is for 4–6 servings the calorie count of the smaller portions is given.

Soups and Appetizers

There is no reason why slimmers should say 'no' to a soup or appetizer, as long as it is relatively low in calories, and it can make an interesting beginning to a calorie-counted meal. Just make sure that subsequent courses don't push your daily allowance over the top.

Avoid soups that have been thickened, and choose clear soups or those that thicken naturally from the ingredients included in the recipe. Eat crispbread as an accompaniment, avoiding other breads and croûtons. Chopped hard-boiled egg white makes an attractive garnish for many soups, without pushing up the calories.

Hors d'oeuvre can be packed full of calories, particularly rich pâtés, and those with heavy sauces. Generally speaking, the simpler the hors d'oeuvre, as far as ingredients are concerned, the lower it is in calories. Items such as melon, grapefruit, tomato and onion salad, and asparagus are ideal as low-calorie appetizers.

CHINESE-STYLE VEGETABLE SOUP (*Photograph by American Rice Council*)

Chinese-Style Vegetable Soup

Approx. 60 calories per portion

1 tablespoon corn oil or olive oil
3 tablespoons long grain rice
2 pints (5 cups) chicken stock,
   or water and 2–3 chicken stock
   cubes

seasoning
1 small carrot
1 small turnip
small piece swede
1–2 sticks celery
Garnish:
chopped parsley

Heat the oil in a saucepan. Add the rice and turn in the oil for several minutes. Pour the stock into the pan, or the water and stock cubes, bring to the boil. Stir briskly, add seasoning. Lower the heat and cover the pan. Simmer gently for 20 minutes, until the rice is just tender.
Grate the vegetables finely or coarsely according to personal taste, add to the soup and heat for a few minutes only so the vegetables retain their firm texture. Add extra seasoning if required. Serve topped with parsley.
Serves 4–6.

Variation:
Add yogurt to the soup just before serving.

Rice and Lemon Soup

Approx. 45 calories per portion

2 pints (5 cups) chicken stock
3 tablespoons long grain rice
1 or 2 lemons

seasoning
Garnish:
chopped parsley

Simmer the stock with the rice, lemon juice and $\frac{1}{2}$–1 teaspoon finely grated lemon rind for 20–25 minutes. Season well and top with parsley.
Serves 4–6.

Onion and Pepper Soup

Approx. 50 calories per portion

2 large onions
1–2 cloves garlic (optional)
1 oz. (2 tablespoons) butter or
  margarine
1 large green and 1 large red
  pepper
1½ pints (3¾ cups) brown or white
  stock or water

2 large tomatoes
2–4 oz. (½–1 cup) mushrooms
seasoning
Garnish:
chopped herbs
grated cheese

Peel the onions and cut into narrow strips. Peel and crush the garlic cloves. Heat the butter or margarine gently and toss the onion and garlic in this until nearly transparent. Take care the onions do not brown.

Discard the cores and seeds from the peppers and cut the pulp, or flesh, into small strips. Blend with the onion but do not fry if you like a firm texture.

Add the liquid, bring steadily to the boil. Add the skinned chopped tomatoes and sliced mushrooms. Continue cooking until the vegetables are soft. Season well.

Serve while very hot. Garnish with chopped fresh herbs and grated cheese.
Serves 4–6.

Variations:
Use all onions and brown stock.
Use all mushrooms and brown stock.

Frosted Tomato Cocktail

Approx. 25 calories per portion

Although this cocktail can be served to everyone at the beginning of a meal, without the choice of an alternative, I occasionally have made it part of a mixed hors d'oeuvre, for it balances the rather rich flavour of foods in mayonnaise. In this case scoop out balls of the frosted mixture and serve on a bed of lettuce.

2 lb. ripe tomatoes
4 tablespoons water
seasoning
artificial sweetener to taste

little lemon juice
Worcestershire sauce to taste
Garnish:
lettuce or mint

Chop the tomatoes. Put into a saucepan with the water, seasoning and sweetener. Heat for a few minutes only so you can extract the juice. Rub through a sieve or emulsify. Add lemon juice, Worcestershire sauce and any extra seasoning or flavouring required – celery salt, cayenne pepper and a few drops chilli sauce can be added. Put into the freezing tray and freeze lightly.

Either spoon or scoop on to lettuce leaves and make part of a mixed hors d'oeuvre, or chop lightly and spoon into chilled glasses and top with mint leaves.

Serves 4–6, or 8–12 if part of a mixed hors d'oeuvre.

Variation:

Frosted Melon Cocktail: The red fleshed water melon is ideal. Halve the melon, remove the seeds and scoop out the flesh. Mix with lemon juice, a little sweetener, then taste. You may like to add seasoning to make it more piquant in flavour and/or a few drops chilli or Worcestershire sauce. Freeze and serve as the tomato cocktail above.

To prepare in advance:

This must be prepared early, since it needs time to frost adequately. It can be stored in a freezer or freezing compartment for some time. Do not serve it too cold though.

Economy hint:

When tomatoes are expensive use canned or bottled tomato juice and omit the water.

Chicken Noodle Soup

Approx. 65 calories per portion

carcass of a chicken
about $2\frac{1}{2}$–3 pints ($6\frac{1}{4}$–$7\frac{1}{2}$ cups)
  water to cover
seasoning
1–2 onions
1–2 carrots

bouquet garni
3–4 tablespoons shell noodles
1 oz. ($\frac{1}{4}$ cup) flour

Put the chicken carcass, plus the giblets, less the liver, if
available, into a saucepan. Cover with water, add seasoning,
prepared vegetables and herbs. Bring the liquid to the boil,
cover the pan and simmer for at least 2 hours or, if using a
pressure cooker, allow about 40 minutes at 15 lb. pressure.
Strain the stock. Any small pieces of chicken can be chopped
or sieved and added to the stock just before serving. Add the
noodles and cook steadily for 15 minutes or until tender.
Blend the flour with a little stock, put into the pan with the
remainder of the stock and cook until slightly thickened,
stirring well.
Serves 5–6.

Variations:
Chicken Soup: Ingredients as above but omit the noodles.

Creamy Chicken Soup: Ingredients as above but omit the
noodles and use $1\frac{1}{2}$ pints ($3\frac{3}{4}$ cups) water only. Simmer the
giblets, etc. as above. Strain and sieve any tiny pieces of
chicken and add to the liquid. Blend the flour in the recipe
with $\frac{1}{2}$ pint ($1\frac{1}{4}$ cups) skimmed milk. Stir into the chicken
liquid with 1–2 oz. butter or margarine and cook until
thickened. Taste, add more seasoning if required. Add a little
natural yogurt before serving.

Spiced Fish Soup

Approx. 70 calories per portion

1 tablespoon oil
1–2 cloves garlic
1 large onion
3 large tomatoes
1½ pints (3¾ cups) fish stock
½ teaspoon paprika
pinch allspice
good pinch saffron*

pinch turmeric
about 12 oz. white fish
seasoning
Garnish:
parsley

*If using a few saffron strands instead of saffron powder infuse this in the stock for about 30 minutes, then strain and use the stock.

Heat the oil in a pan, fry the crushed garlic, the chopped onion and skinned chopped tomatoes until a thick purée.
Blend the fish stock with all the flavourings, add to the purée, together with the finely diced, skinned raw white fish.
Simmer until the fish is tender. Season to taste and garnish with parsley just before serving.
Serves 4–6.

Variation:
Genoese fish soup: Follow the recipe above and add a few shelled prawns and mussels just before serving.

To complete the meal:
Serve citrus fruit as the soup is rather rich; either grapefruit before the meal or a salad of orange and grapefruit segments after the soup.

To serve for a buffet:
Flake the fish finely and put bowls of croûtons on the table.

Artichokes Vinaigrette

Approx. 15 calories per portion (excluding oil and vinegar dressing)

artichokes   oil and vinegar dressing,
salt   see below

Wash the artichokes in cold salted water. Cut away any stalk
and pull off any rather tough outer leaves. You can cut the
tops of the leaves in a straight line with scissors, if wished.
Cook the whole artichokes in boiling salted water until
tender. The time varies – small very young artichokes take
about 25 minutes, very large ones take about 40 minutes.
Test to see if you can pull away a leaf.
To serve hot: Drain and serve with a little melted butter.
To serve cold: Make an oil and vinegar dressing using
1 tablespoon oil and 2 tablespoons vinegar, season well and
either spoon into the centre of each artichoke or serve
separately. (This adds an extra 132 calories.)

Note:
If you wish to serve the dressing in the centre of the cold
artichoke, then pull out the centre part of the vegetable. It is
easier to do this when just warm; then allow it to cool.

Asparagus Parmesan

Approx. 160 calories per portion

cooked or canned asparagus   grated Parmesan cheese
little butter

Drain the asparagus and heat gently in a little butter. Arrange
carefully in a flame-proof dish, and top with a thin coating of
Parmesan cheese. Brown under a hot grill (broiler).

Variation:
Asparagus Polanaise: Fry a few coarse breadcrumbs in a
little hot butter, mix with chopped hard boiled eggs and
chopped parsley and/or chopped chives and sprinkle over the
asparagus just before serving.

24

Aubergines Gratinées

Approx. 190 calories per portion

4 small or 2 large aubergines (eggplants)
seasoning
2 tablespoons oil
4 oz. cooked lean ham
2 tablespoons chopped spring onions (scallions)
2 oz. (1 cup) soft breadcrumbs

2 teaspoons chopped parsley
1 teaspoon chopped dill or other herbs
1 egg
Topping:
few crisp breadcrumbs
1 tablespoon melted butter

Wash and halve the aubergines (eggplants) lengthways. Score the skins with a sharp knife, sprinkle with salt and leave for about 20 minutes. This lessens the slightly bitter taste, that many people dislike. Heat the oil in a pan and fry the aubergines (eggplants) on both sides until nearly cooked.
Lift out of the pan and arrange in a shallow oven-proof dish, cut side uppermost.
Chop the ham very finely, mix with the spring onions (scallions), breadcrumbs, herbs and egg. Season well and spread this over the top of the halved aubergines (eggplants). Sprinkle crisp breadcrumbs over and moisten with melted butter. Bake for 25 minutes in the centre of a moderate oven, 350°F, Gas Mark 4.
Serves 4.

Variations:
Top the aubergines (eggplants) with a little grated Parmesan cheese instead of the crisp breadcrumbs.
Use minced chicken or other meat in place of ham.
Fry tomatoes until a thick purée, seasoning well. Spread over the halved partially cooked aubergines (eggplants), then put on the topping as the basic recipe or one of the variations and bake as in the basic recipe.

To serve for a buffet:
Although the recipe is excellent for a buffet the aubergines (eggplants) are a little difficult to cut with a fork. Slice the aubergines (eggplants), fry, then put into the dish, spoon the topping over and bake.

Beans Niçoise

Approx. 100 calories per portion

1 lb. green beans
seasoning
Sauce:
1 lb. tomatoes
1 clove garlic

1 small onion
2 tablespoons oil
2 tablespoons chopped parsley

If using runner beans, slice in the usual way. French and haricot verts can be left whole, just remove the ends and string the sides if necessary. Cook in a little well seasoned water until nearly tender.

Meanwhile skin and chop the tomatoes, crush the garlic and chop the onion. Fry the onion and garlic in the hot oil in another saucepan, add the tomatoes and cook for a few minutes.

Strain the beans, save about $\frac{1}{4}$ pint ($\frac{2}{3}$ cup) of the liquid from the pan and tip this and the beans into the tomato mixture. Finish cooking, season to taste and top with the parsley.
Serves 4.

To complete the meal:
The vegetable course would be very satisfying, so follow with cheese and fruit.

To serve for a buffet:
Although this dish and the variations taste delicious they do not look particularly exciting for a buffet party.

Walnut and Avocado Salad

Approx. 230 calories per portion

2 ripe avocado pears
a little lemon juice
2 crisp, sweep apples

2 oz. ($\frac{1}{3}$ cup) chopped walnuts
oil and vinegar dressing (see
    page 24)

Choose ripe but firm avocados – shake to see if the stone moves. Carefully cut avocados in half and remove the stones. Scrape the avocado flesh into a bowl, without damaging the skins. Mash with lemon juice – this prevents the avocado turning brown. Peel, core and chop the apples. Mix the apple and nuts with the avocado.

To make the oil and vinegar dressing use four times the amount of ingredients given on page 24. Shake the ingredients together vigorously in a screw-top jar and add to the fruit.

Mix together well and spoon back into the avocado skins. Serve immediately, with crispbread.

Serves 4.

As a main course:

Instead of serving in the avocado skins, pile the mixture on to a bed of crisp lettuce, surrounded with sliced cucumber, strips of green pepper and celery sticks. Garnish with extra walnut pieces or hard boiled eggs, cut in half. Serve chilled.

Vegetables and Salads

Vegetables and salads are a boon to slimmers, as they help add colour, variety and texture to a diet. Apart from the very starchy vegetables such as potatoes and swedes, most can be eaten regularly in a calorie-controlled diet. Check their appropriate calorific values on the chart to give an idea of portion sizes.

Always cook vegetables in as little liquid as possible, to retain the maximum amount of flavour, texture and nutritive value. The use of stock, rather than water, will add extra flavour. If you want to top vegetables with 'an extra something' in place of butter, use a low-fat spread, which is only half the calories per ounce. Ratatouille (page 32) is one of the most delicious of vegetable dishes.

Salads add a crisp refreshing contrast to many main meals, and such a wide variety of different ingredients can be used as shown in the salad on the jacket, which combines white cabbage, peppers, mushrooms, celery, radishes, cucumber and cauliflower with grapefruit and orange rind. Dressings can be the downfall of an otherwise low-calorie salad. If you really like an oil and vinegar dressing, then use more vinegar than oil, flavoured with mustard and artificial sweetener, and *use sparingly.* Or mix thin low-fat natural yogurt with lemon or orange juice, and flavour with salt and pepper, garlic, mustard or herbs. Try Grapefruit Jellied Salad (page 34) for a totally different type of salad.

Courgettes à la Provençale

Approx. 32 calories per portion

1 lb. ripe tomatoes
1–2 cloves garlic
1 onion
little stock or water

1 lb. courgettes (zucchini)
seasoning

Skin and chop the tomatoes and put into the pan with the crushed garlic and very finely diced onion. Add a little stock, chicken for preference, or water, and simmer until a thin purée. Slice the courgettes (zucchini) thinly, add to the purée, with a generous amount of seasoning and simmer steadily for about 30 minutes until tender. If the purée of tomatoes seems too thin lift the lid of the pan, so excess liquid can evaporate, but watch that the mixture does not stick to the bottom of the pan.
Gives generous portions for 4.

Variation:
Richer version: Toss the sliced courgettes (zucchini) in a little oil before adding the crushed garlic and onions. Fry until the courgettes (zucchini) are very pale golden coloured, then add the tomatoes, stock or water and seasoning. This version makes a better hors d'oeuvre.

To prepare in advance:
Make either version and put into a casserole and heat through gently.

Economy hint:
Use diced marrow (squash) instead of the more expensive courgettes. When marrows (squash) are very young there is no need to remove either the peel or the barely formed seeds.

New way to serve:
If you add diced lean bacon, fried until crisp, or diced cooked ham, chopped parsley and a little chopped lemon thyme this makes an excellent dressing for chicken and there is no need to make either a stuffing or a sauce.

Ratatouille

Approx. 112 calories per portion

1 medium-sized to large aubergine (eggplant)
about 8 oz. courgettes (zucchini)
seasoning
1 lb. ripe tomatoes
4 medium-sized onions

1–2 cloves garlic
1 green pepper
1 red pepper
2 tablespoons olive oil
Garnish:
chopped or sprigged parsley, optional

If you dislike the taste of the peel on an aubergine (eggplant) remove this, otherwise dice the vegetable neatly with the peel on. Slice the courgettes (zucchini). Put the vegetables into a bowl, sprinkle lightly with salt and pepper, leave for 30 minutes. This minimizes the bitter taste from the aubergine (eggplant) peel, and draws out the water from the courgettes. Skin and slice or chop the tomatoes and onions; chop or crush the cloves of garlic. Dice the flesh from the pepper, discarding the cores and seeds.

Heat the olive oil in a pan, add the tomatoes and onions and cook gently for a few minutes, to let the juice flow from the tomatoes. This makes sure the mixture will not stick to the pan. Add the rest of the vegetables, and stir well. Season and cover the pan with a tightly fitting lid. Simmer gently until as tender as you would wish, about 30 minutes in all. Serve hot.

If you wish this to be a cold hors d'oeuvre, then I suggest cooking them a little longer until quite soft. Top with parsley before serving.
Serves 4–6.

Variations:
The recipe uses the minimum of oil, you may prefer to use a little more. Add 3–4 tablespoons chopped parsley, or parsley and chives to the vegetables before cooking.

Cook in a tightly covered casserole for at least 45 minutes in a moderately hot oven, 375°F, Mark 5, or 1 hour in a slow oven, 300°F, Mark 2.

The proportions of vegetables are entirely a matter of personal taste. Add sliced mushrooms if wished and omit the pepper.

Grapefruit Jellied Salad

Approx. 120 calories per portion

2 grapefruit
$\frac{1}{4}$ pint ($\frac{2}{3}$ cup) low calorie salad
  dressing
4 teaspoons gelatine
$\frac{1}{2}$ pint ($1\frac{1}{4}$ cups) tomato juice

4 oz. cooked lean ham, cut in
  1 thick slice
seasoning
mixed salad

Halve one grapefruit and squeeze out all the juice, make up
to $\frac{1}{4}$ pint ($\frac{2}{3}$ cup) with water. Halve the other grapefruit and
spoon out the segments carefully discarding pips and skin,
blend these with the salad dressing.
Soften the gelatine in a little cold tomato juice then dissolve
in the remaining hot tomato juice. Allow to cool, then blend
with the grapefruit juice. Leave until the mixture just starts
to stiffen, then fold in the grapefruit and salad dressing and
the neatly diced ham. Taste the mixture and add seasoning if
required, some people may like a little sugar. Put into an
oiled $1\frac{1}{2}$–2 pint (4–5 cup) mould and leave until firm. Turn
out on to a bed of mixed salad.
Serves 4–6.

Variations:
Use the grapefruit salad above and add whole or chopped
prawns in place of the ham.
Use 2–3 pineapple rings instead of the grapefruit segments
and pineapple juice instead of grapefruit juice. This makes a
sweeter salad, which also blends well with ham or lean
cooked pork.
Children may enjoy the refreshing flavour of this salad but it
is generally a more adult taste.

Tuna Salad

Flake tuna fish, and mix with low calorie salad dressing, diced cucumber, or gherkins when cucumber is expensive, and coarsely chopped hard boiled eggs. Arrange in a ring of watercress or shredded green lettuce or other greens. Top with more chopped hard boiled egg. Canned salmon or cooked white fish may be used instead of tuna, but flavour the dressing with either a little anchovy essence, or tomato purée, or ketchup.

Savoury Tongue Salad

Tongue is a fairly expensive meat so make it go further in the following way:
Blend diced green pepper (discard the core and seeds) and equal quantities of a fairly sweet pickle and low calorie salad dressing. Spread over slices of cooked tongue. Roll lightly and arrange on a bed of mixed salad.

Coleslaw

Approx. 20 calories per portion

Never worry unduly if your children do not like cooked cabbage, serve it raw (when it retains the maximum of mineral salts and vitamins) in a cabbage salad – generally called a coleslaw. Remember, prolonged soaking allows these precious salts and vitamins to be wasted so do not prepare too long before serving.

heart of a small white cabbage	1 tablespoon vinegar
3 large carrots	low calorie salad dressing
	little chopped parsley

Wash, dry and shred the cabbage very finely. Grate the peeled carrots. Put into a bowl with the cabbage, then add the vinegar and enough dressing to bind. Add a little chopped parsley to the salad and top with extra parsley just before serving.
Serves 6–8.

Fried Beans

Approx. 42 calories per portion

1 onion, thinly sliced
1 clove garlic, crushed
1 tablespoon olive oil
1 lb. green beans
1 large tomato

1 hot chilli, finely chopped
1 tablespoon sugar
salt
1 tablespoon coconut cream (see below)

Fry the sliced onion and crushed garlic in oil. Add the coarsely chopped beans, peeled tomato, minute pieces of chilli, sugar and salt to taste. Stir until glazed.
Cover the pan tightly and simmer gently for about 20 minutes, until the beans are tender.
Add the coconut cream and stir until heated through. Serve immediately.
Serves 4.

Coconut cream is made by pouring hot skimmed milk over desiccated coconut and mixing to a liquid in an electric blender.

Fish

There is a wide variety of fish available, and it is important for slimmers to know which ones they can choose happily to fit into a diet. The oilier the fish is in texture, the higher it is in calories. White fish is the best choice, and it has a relatively low calorie count.

The one advantage fish has over many other foods is that it can be cooked simply, without the addition of other high-calorie ingredients, to provide some delicious dishes.

Grilling, poaching, steaming and baking are the most suitable low-calorie methods for cooking fish. It can be steamed over a pan of boiling water, between two plates; grilled or baked in the oven, with a topping of low-fat spread; or poached in stock, water, skimmed milk, or a little dry white wine.

Three recipes for slightly more elaborate fish dishes follow, and the Chaudfroid of Fish (page 40) makes a delicious dish for summer.

Savoury Grilled (Broiled) Turbot

Approx. 270 calories per portion

2 oz. ($\frac{1}{4}$ cup) butter
1 tablespoon lemon juice
$\frac{1}{2}$–1 teaspoon paprika
seasoning

4 steaks turbot or other white fish
Garnish:
parsley, lemon

Heat the butter in a pan until it turns golden brown. This gives a delicious flavour to the fish, but it is essential the butter does not become too dark. Add the lemon juice, paprika and seasoning. Brush one side of the fish with some

of the butter mixture and put on the greased grill (broiler) pan or foil. Cook under the heated grill (broiler) until just tender (do not over-cook), turning once.
Serve topping with any remaining hot butter and garnish with parsley and lemon.
Serves 4.

Chaudfroid of Fish

Approx. 244 calories per portion

This creamy coating can be used on cooked salmon, salmon trout, or even fillets of sole or plaice, although the latter are less inviting in a cold salad. Do not over-cook fish if serving this as a cold dish, for the fish continues to soften as it cools.

Chaudfroid Sauce for coating for 6–8 portions:
aspic jelly powder to set ½ pint (1¼ cups) water
1 level teaspoon powdered gelatine
½ pint (1¼ cups) water

½ pint (1¼ cups) low calorie salad dressing
6–8 portions cooked fish
Garnish:
cucumber, etc.
lettuce
lemon

Mix the aspic jelly and powdered gelatine together, soften in a little cold water, then heat the remainder of the water and dissolve the softened aspic and powdered gelatine in this. Allow to cool, and then blend with the low calorie salad dressing. Allow the mixture to stiffen very slightly.

Arrange the pieces of fish on a wire cooling tray and coat with the Chaudfroid sauce. Press tiny pieces of cucumber, radish, pepper, tomato to form an attractive design on top of the sauce. When quite firm lift on to a bed of lettuce and garnish with lemon.
Serves 6–8.

Note: Put a large dish under the wire cooling tray, so any surplus sauce drops on to this.

Variation:
Chaudfroid mould of fish: Make the mixture as the coating above. When cool add approximately 1–1¼ lb. well drained canned or cooked flaked fish – white fish, salmon, shell fish or use a mixture of fish. Put into an oiled mould and leave to set. Turn out on to a bed of mixed salad.

Haddock Soufflé

Approx. 200 calories per portion

Béchamel sauce:
piece carrot
piece celery
½ pint (1¼ cups) skimmed milk
1 oz. (2 tablespoons) butter
1 oz. (¼ cup) flour

seasoning
8 oz. cooked fresh or smoked
   haddock
4 eggs

Put the carrot and celery in the milk. Warm gently for a few minutes then allow the pan to stand in a warm place for a time so the milk absorbs the flavour of the vegetables. Strain the milk. When making a coating Béchamel sauce measure the liquid and make up to ½ pint (1¼ cups) again. When using the Béchamel sauce for this soufflé, do not use any more milk. Heat the butter in a large pan, stir in the flour, then cook for 2–3 minutes. Gradually work in the strained milk, bring to the boil and cook until thickened. Season well, add the flaked fish, the egg yolks, and then the stiffly whisked egg whites. Put into a greased soufflé dish and bake in the centre of a moderate oven, 350–375°F, Mark 4–5, for 35 minutes, until golden brown and well risen. Serve at once.
Serves 6 as an hors d'oeuvre or 3 as a light main course.

Variations:
Use about 6 oz. (¾ cup) flaked cooked or canned tuna or salmon.
For a firmer textured soufflé use only 7½ fluid oz. (barely 1 cup) milk for the Béchamel sauce.
A soufflé sinks less if you omit the egg yolks and use only the egg whites, so try this version, which serves a smaller number of portions, for parties.

To prepare in advance:
Make the sauce then leave it in the saucepan, and cover with damp greaseproof (waxed) paper to prevent a skin forming. Prepare the fish.

Meat and Poultry

Cooking meat and poultry provides many problems for slimmers, as so many main dishes involve pastry, a coating of egg and breadcrumbs, or a thick sauce. As with fish, the simpler the cooking method, the kinder it is to the waistline. This means avoiding pies, meat and poultry that has been coated and deep fried, and thickened casseroles and stews. This still leaves many exciting and tasty meat and poultry dishes for those on a diet. As a quick guide, lamb and pork are two of the meats highest in calories, whereas chicken, turkey and veal are relatively low. (Veal has a calorie count of only 31 per ounce.) Always choose lean meat, and remove the skin from poultry and game before eating. Sausages of all varieties are best avoided, as they contain cereals and other 'extenders'.

The many recipes in this section can provide the focal point of memorable low-calorie meals which family and friends, as well as slimmers, can enjoy. The dishes range from a simple Braised Beef Neapolitan (page 46), to a more elaborate recipe for Hare in Madeira Sauce (page 52).

Veal Fricasseé

Approx. 273 calories per portion

1 onion, chopped
2 carrots, peeled and chopped
2 oz. button mushrooms
½ pint (1¼ cups) water
1 tablespoon lemon juice

½ chicken stock cube
8 oz. pie veal
1 egg yolk
2 tablespoons skimmed milk
salt and pepper

Put the onion, carrots, mushrooms, water, lemon juice and stock
cube into a saucepan and bring to the boil. Cut the veal into
1-inch pieces and add to the boiling mixture. Lower the heat,
cover and simmer gently for about 45 minutes, or until the veal is
tender. Blend the egg yolk with the milk in a basin. Add 3
tablespoons of the hot veal stock, then add to the pan. Stir,
without allowing the mixture to boil, until slightly thickened.
Adjust seasoning and serve.
Serves 2.

Spatchcock of Chicken

Approx. 310 calories per portion

4 very small young chickens or
   2 larger ones
seasoning
1 oz. (2 tablespoons) butter

grated rind 1 lemon
Garnish:
watercress
lemon

Split the chickens right down the backbone, so they open out
quite flat. Mix the seasoning with the melted butter, add the
lemon rind. Grill (broil) the chickens until tender, basting with
the butter. Garnish with watercress and sliced lemon.
Serves 4.

Variation:
Very young pigeons or partridges may be cooked in the same
way. Omit the lemon if wished and flavour the butter with a
few drops Worcestershire sauce and a pinch curry powder.

Dry Chicken Curry with Yellow Rice

Approx. 380 calories per portion (including rice)

½ oz. (1 tablespoon) butter
1 large onion, chopped
1 green pepper, sliced
1 clove garlic, crushed
about 1 tablespoon Madras
  curry powder
1 teaspoon chilli powder
salt
4 chicken joints
4 tomatoes
2 tablespoons yogurt

For the rice:
½ oz. (1 tablespoon) butter
6 oz. (¾ cup) long grain
  refined rice
1 teaspoon turmeric
few cloves
1 teaspoon ground cumin
salt
1 pint (2½ cups) water

Heat the butter in a pan and gently fry the onion, pepper and garlic for about 5 minutes. Add the curry powder, chilli powder and salt and mix well. Add the chicken joints to the pan and brown quickly over a high heat. Lower the heat, cover and simmer gently for 1 hour. If using frozen chicken joints, you will probably not need to add any water at all, but if using fresh joints, add 2–3 tablespoons water before lowering the heat. Add the tomatoes to the pan 5 minutes before the end of the cooking time. Stir in the yogurt just before serving.

Heat the butter for the rice in a pan, and toss the rice gently in this for 5 minutes. Add the spices and salt and mix well. Pour in the water. Cover and simmer gently for about 15 minutes or until the rice is tender and all the liquid absorbed. Before serving the rice can be garnished with a few pieces of sliced cucumber, as in the picture. Serve the curry with the rice, sliced onion, peanuts, chutney and poppadums if liked.

Serves 4.

Braised Beef Neapolitan

Approx. 374 calories per portion

12 oz. good quality, lean
   braising steak
salt and pepper
8 oz. tomatoes

1 small onion, chopped
1 clove garlic, crushed
1 bay leaf
pinch mixed dried herbs

Divide the meat into 2 steaks and cut off any excess fat. Season with salt and pepper. Put under a hot grill (broiler) for about 5 minutes on each side, so it becomes lightly browned. Place in a casserole. Skin the tomatoes; either hold on a fork over a gas flame and remove and peel when the skin bursts, or put into a basin, cover with boiling water for 1 minute, drain and skin. Chop the tomatoes and put into a basin with the onion, garlic, herbs and seasoning. Mix lightly and spoon over the meat. Bake in a moderate oven, 350°F., Gas Mark 4 for 1–2 hours or until the meat is tender. This will depend on the thickness and quality of the meat. Serve with cooked spinach or a green salad.
Serves 2.

Oriental Chicken

Approx. 230 calories per portion

1 large roasting chicken*
Stuffing and sauce:
small can bean sprouts
4 oz. lean ham
small can water chestnuts
1 oz ($\frac{1}{4}$ cup) chopped nuts
seasoning

2 tablespoons chopped preserved
  ginger
$\frac{3}{4}$ pint (2 cups) chicken stock
2 tablespoons cornflour
  (cornstarch)
little oil

*A boiling fowl is unsuitable for this particular dish.

Wash and dry the chicken. Drain the bean sprouts, mix half with the diced ham. Drain and chop half the water chestnuts and add to the ham and bean sprouts, together with the chopped nuts, seasoning and half the ginger. Stuff the chicken with this mixture.

Blend the stock with the cornflour (cornstarch) in a pan. Heat until thickened, stirring well. Add the remainder of the bean sprouts, sliced water chestnuts and ginger, together with a little seasoning and sherry. Pour this mixture into a large casserole. Place the chicken in the casserole. Brush the breast of the bird with oil and cover the casserole with a lid. Cook for 2 hours in the centre of a very moderate to moderate oven, 325–350°F, Mark 3–4.
Serves 6.

Variation:
Although the chicken looks much more impressive stuffed and served whole, it is more difficult to serve. You may care to make the stuffing as the basic recipe, then put this into a covered dish and cook it for about 1 hour in the centre of a very moderate oven, 325–350°F, Mark 3–4. Put 6–8 chicken joints, browned in a little oil, on top of the bean sprout mixture in the casserole and cook in a very moderate oven for 1 hour only.
Either spoon the stuffing round the edge of the casserole before serving or put the same dish on to the table.

To prepare in advance:
Prepare the sauce and stuffing beforehand, do not cook the chicken and reheat it.

Sweet and Sour Chicken Salad

Approx. 191 calories per portion

1 small cooked chicken
Marinade:
2 teaspoons French mustard
4 tablespoons white wine vinegar
6 tablespoons low calorie salad
  dressing
2 cloves garlic
1 teaspoon soy sauce
1 tablespoon honey
seasoning

about 8 small pickled gherkins or
  2 larger pickled cucumbers
4 rings pineapple
1 tablespoon raisins
2 tablespoons blanched flaked
  almonds
Garnish:
endive (chicory) or lettuce
sliced beetroot
sliced cooked potatoes

Cut the chicken into small neat pieces. Blend the mustard with
the white wine vinegar (if not obtainable use half white wine
and half white malt vinegar), then add the dressing, crushed
garlic, soy sauce, honey and seasoning. Add the sliced
gherkins or pickled cucumbers and diced pineapple, raisins
and the pieces of chicken. Allow to stand for only 15 minutes.
If the chicken has not absorbed all the marinade then spoon
this out of the bowl and sprinkle over the salad at the last
minute. Stir the nuts into the mixture just before serving.
Arrange the endive (chicory) or lettuce on a dish, pile the
chicken mixture in the centre and the sliced beetroot and
potatoes around the edge of the dish.
Serves 6.

Note: The vinegar will make the chicken over-soft, so do not
prepare too soon before serving.

Variations:
Use lean cooked pork or cooked ham instead of the chicken
and add a good pinch curry powder and a little lemon juice to
the low calorie salad dressing.

Simple Pot-au-Feu

Approx. 340 calories per portion

1 tablespoon oil
1 onion, chopped
2 carrots, chopped
2 leeks, cleaned and chopped
2 sticks celery, chopped
8 oz. stewing beef
1 tablespoon flour

1 tablespoon concentrated
  tomato purée
½ pint (1¼ cups) water
1 beef stock cube
salt and pepper
4 oz. potatoes

Heat the oil in a pan and fry the onion, carrots, leeks and celery for about 5 minutes. Cut the beef into 1-inch cubes and fry with the vegetables for 5 minutes. Sprinkle over the flour and cook, stirring, for 2 minutes. Add the tomato purée, and gradually stir in the water. Bring to the boil, stirring all the time. Add the stock cube and seasoning. Cover and simmer for 2 hours. Peel the potatoes and cut into ½-inch slices. Add to the pan and cook for a further 30 minutes.
Serves 2.

To vary: Other vegetables such as turnips, peas and mushrooms could be used instead of those given here.
Bedsitter cooks: These one-pot stews and casseroles are ideal if you have only one gas ring.

Tajine Tfaia (Moroccan Lamb Dish)

Approx. 340 calories per portion

$1\frac{1}{4}$–$1\frac{1}{2}$ lb. lean lamb – cut from
  the top of the leg if possible
good pinch cumin
pinch powdered saffron
pinch ginger
seasoning
finely grated rind 1–2 lemons
1 oz. (2 tablespoons) butter

2 onions
1 clove garlic
little water or stock
about 1 tablespoon lemon juice
1 oz. ($\frac{1}{4}$ cup) blanched almonds

Cut the lamb into small cubes, about 1–$1\frac{1}{2}$-inches in size. Mix
the spices with seasoning and lemon rind and roll the meat in
this. Heat the butter gently in a tajine or in a heat-proof dish,
or strong pan with a lid. Cook the lamb until it turns golden
brown on the outside. Add the finely chopped onions,
crushed garlic and just enough water or stock to prevent the
mixture becoming dry. Cover the cooking utensil and simmer
for about 10–15 minutes, until the meat and vegetables are
tender and moist – there should be no surplus liquid. Add
the lemon juice, any extra seasoning required and the
almonds. Heat for a few minutes and serve.
This is excellent with a little rice or the coarse semolina
known as cous-cous.
Serves 4–6.

Variation:
Use chicken instead of lamb. If the chicken joints are small do
not bone these. If preferred bone before cooking, then cut the
chicken into 1–$1\frac{1}{2}$-inch pieces. Since the dish looks whiter
with chicken you may wish to brown the blanched almonds
before adding to the mixture.

To prepare in advance:
The Tajine Tfaia – whether made with lamb or chicken – can
be cooked, and then warmed through gently in the oven.
Cook and rinse the rice, and warm on a flat dish, covering
with greased greaseproof (waxed) paper so it does not dry.

Hare in Madeira Sauce

Approx. 275 calories per portion

1 jointed young hare
½ oz. (2 tablespoons) flour
little chopped sage
2 oz. (¼ cup) butter or cooking fat
4 oz. (1 cup) button mushrooms

12 tablespoons (1 cup) Madeira
 wine
good pinch dried or ½ teaspoon
 freshly chopped herbs
seasoning

If wishing to serve 4 people only, use just the saddle of the
hare. If wishing to serve up to 8 people, use all the hare and
double all the ingredients in the recipe.

Sprinkle the saddle joints of hare with flour, mixed with a
little chopped sage. Heat half the butter or cooking fat and
brown the hare in this. Lift out of the pan and put into a
casserole. Heat the rest of the butter or cooking fat and cook
the mushrooms in this. Add to the casserole with the wine,
herbs and seasoning. Cover the casserole. Allow 1 hour in a
moderate to moderately hot oven, 375–400°F, Mark 5–6.
Serves 4.

Casserole of Hare:

Simmer the liver of the hare to make a good flavoured stock.
Make a brown sauce with 1 oz. (2 tablespoons) butter,
1 oz. (¼ cup) flour, the stock, add seasoning, 2 tablespoons
red currant jelly and ¼ pint (⅔ cup) red wine. Fry the whole
jointed hare in a little cooking fat, drain, then fry 12 small
onions. Put the hare and onions into a casserole, top with the
sauce and cover, then cook for about 3 hours in a very
moderate oven, 325–350°F, Mark 3–4.

Goulash of Gulyas
(Hungarian Paprika Stew)

Approx. 340 calories per portion

12 oz. lean beef – choose good
    quality chuck steak
12 oz. stewing veal or lean pork
2–3 onions
1 oz. (2 tablespoons) butter
seasoning

about 3 teaspoons paprika – use
    less the first time to make sure
    you enjoy the flavour
1–1½ lb. tomatoes
little water or white stock
Garnish:
soured cream
parsley

Cut the meat into neat pieces, peel and slice the onions neatly. Heat the butter in a pan with a tightly fitting lid – this is important for a goulash is a thick stew with little extra liquid. Fry the meat in the hot butter until golden coloured, add the onions, seasoning and paprika, and stir well to blend. Skin and slice the tomatoes, put into the pan with a few tablespoons water or stock. Cover the pan and simmer very gently until the meat is tender. This will be about 1½–2 hours. If necessary, add a little liquid during cooking. Turn into a serving dish and top with soured cream and parsley.
Serve with noodles and salad.
Serves 4–6.

Variations:
Other meat or diced uncooked chicken may be used instead of beef and veal.
This stew has a sweet, not a hot flavour, so most people would enjoy it, even if they do not like curry.

To prepare in advance:
Either prepare beforehand and allow to cook for the time given in the basic recipe in the centre of a very moderate oven, 325–350°F, Mark 3–4, or cook and reheat.

Wiener Schnitzel

Approx. 279 calories per portion

4 escalopes veal or pork
seasoning
1 tablespoon flour
1 egg

3–4 tablespoons fine soft
   breadcrumbs
2 oz. ($\frac{1}{4}$ cup) butter
1 lemon
little chopped parsley

The meat must be very thin, so flatten with a rolling pin if
necessary. Coat the slices of meat in seasoned flour, then
beaten egg and breadcrumbs. Heat the butter very gently in
the pan. Add the meat and cook quickly on one side, turn
with tongs or two knives (do not pierce with the prongs of a
fork as this allows the meat juices to escape). Fry quickly on
the second side, lower the heat and continue cooking for a
total time of about 10 minutes only.
Garnish with slices of lemon and chopped parsley. If the lemon
and parsley are put on the meat *in* the pan and warmed for
1–2 minutes, the maximum flavour can be extracted. For a
more elaborate garnish top the lemon slices with chopped
hard boiled eggs, capers and anchovy fillets.
Serves 4.

Variations:
If you buy very small pieces of veal and serve 2–3 per person
the cooking time is even shorter than the time taken in the
above recipe.
Veal in paprika sauce: Do not coat the veal, fry in butter as
instructions above. Remove the veal when tender. Blend
2 teaspoons paprika (a sweet, not hot flavouring) with a shake
of cayenne pepper and $\frac{1}{4}$ pint ($\frac{2}{3}$ cup) natural yogurt and stir
into the pan, absorbing all the meat juice. A very little dry
sherry can also be added. Heat gently, pour over the veal.

Lemon and Ginger Chops

Approx. 441 calories per portion

1 tablespoon oil
grated rind of 1 lemon
2 tablespoons lemon juice
1 tablespoon brown sugar

$1\frac{1}{2}$ teaspoons ground ginger
salt and pepper
2 large or 4 smaller chump or
    loin chops

Mix the oil, lemon rind, lemon juice, brown sugar, ground ginger and seasoning together. Place the chops in a shallow dish and pour the marinade over them. Leave for 2–3 hours, or up to 36 hours, turning occasionally. Remove the chops and place under a hot grill (broiler). Cook for 15 minutes, turning the chops once and basting them with the marinade. Garnish with lemon and parsley if wished.

Serves 2.

LEMON AND GINGER CHOPS (*Photograph by New Zealand Lamb Information Bureau*)

Somerset Pork

Approx. 403 calories per portion

1–1¼ lb. pork fillet (tenderloin)
1 tablespoon flour
1 oz. (2 tablespoons) butter
1 large onion, finely chopped
6 oz. (1½ cups) mushrooms, sliced

½ pint (1¼ cups) dry cider
salt and pepper
4 tablespoons natural yogurt
Garnish:
chopped parsley

Cut the pork fillet into 8 pieces. Place each piece between 2 sheets of greaseproof (waxed) paper, and beat with a meat hammer or a wooden rolling pin until it is ¼ inch thick. Coat the pork lightly with the flour. Melt the butter and fry the pork slowly for about 4 minutes on each side. Remove from the pan, drain well and keep warm. Add the onions and mushrooms to the pan, and cook gently until tender, but not brown. Stir in the remaining flour, and cook for a minute. Remove from the heat and gradually stir in the cider. Return to the heat and bring to the boil, stirring. Add the pork and seasoning, then stir in the yogurt. Heat for a further 2–3 minutes *without boiling*. Serve garnished with chopped parsley.
Serves 4.

Devilled Chicken

Approx. 262 calories per portion

3 tablespoons chutney
1 tablespoon concentrated
   tomato purée
$\frac{1}{4}$ teaspoon Tabasco sauce

$\frac{1}{4}$ teaspoon made mustard
salt and pepper
4 small chicken joints

Put the chutney, tomato purée, Tabasco sauce, mustard and seasoning into a basin. Mix well together. Brush the mixture over the chicken joints, or make two or three deep slits in each chicken joint and fill with the devilled mixture. Place in a roasting tin and cover with foil. Bake in a moderately hot oven, 400°F., Gas Mark 6 for about 45 minutes. Uncover and continue cooking for a further 10–15 minutes or until the chicken is tender.
Serves 4.

Liver Ragoût

Approx. 199 calories per portion

1 onion, sliced
2 carrots, sliced
1 small turnip, chopped
$\frac{1}{2}$ pint ($1\frac{1}{4}$ cups) water
1 beef stock cube
2 teaspoons Worcestershire
   sauce

salt
8 oz. lamb's liver, thinly sliced
about $\frac{1}{4}$ pint ($\frac{2}{3}$ cup) skimmed
   milk

Put the onion, carrots, turnip, water, stock cube, Worcestershire sauce and salt into a saucepan, cover, bring to the boil and simmer for 30 minutes. Meanwhile cut the liver into thin strips and soak in a little skimmed milk (this removes the slightly bitter flavour from the liver). Drain the liver and add to the vegetables in the pan. Simmer for about 10 minutes or until the liver is tender. Taste and adjust seasoning.
Serves 2.

Lamb Shish-Kebabs with Herbed Sauce

Approx. 400 calories per portion

Sauce:
about ½ pint (1¼ cups) tomato
  juice
2 teaspoons made mustard
¼ pint (⅔ cup) natural yogurt
shake cayenne pepper
2 teaspoons finely chopped mint
2 teaspoons chopped chives or
  spring onions

seasoning
¼ teaspoon ground cinnamon
Kebabs:
1 lb. lean lamb (cut from the leg)
1 green pepper
8–12 button mushrooms
4 small tomatoes
12 small cocktail onions
1 oz. (2 tablespoons) butter
seasoning

Mix all the ingredients for the sauce. Put into a shallow dish.
Cut the lamb into 1-inch cubes. Put into the sauce and leave
for 3–4 hours, turn several times. Lift the meat out of the
sauce.
Cut the flesh of the green pepper into 8–12 pieces, discard the
core and seeds. Thread the meat and vegetables on to 4 long
metal skewers. Brush the vegetables, but not the meat, with
the melted butter, season lightly. Cook under a hot grill
(broiler), turning several times, until tender. Brush the meat
once or twice with the sauce. Heat the remaining sauce
gently and serve with the kebabs. Serve with a little boiled
rice.
Serves 4.

Variations:
Sausage kebabs: Use small sausages instead of diced lamb.
Kidney kebabs: Skin and halve lambs' kidneys (use instead
of the lamb) and brush with melted butter or add small rolls
of bacon to the skewers.

To complete the meal:
Serve with green salad.

Coq au Vin

Approx. 334 calories per portion

2–4 oz. small mushrooms
1 oz. (2 tablespoons) butter or
   margarine
1 tablespoon flour
$\frac{1}{2}$ pint ($1\frac{1}{4}$ cups) white wine or
   use half wine and half chicken
   stock*

2–3 tablespoons cocktail onions
seasoning
1 cooked chicken
Garnish:
chopped parsley

*or water and $\frac{1}{4}-\frac{1}{2}$ chicken stock cube.

Toss the mushrooms in the hot butter or margarine. Blend the flour with the wine, add to the mushrooms and stir gently until thickened. Put in the well drained onions, a little seasoning and simmer for a few minutes. Meanwhile, heat the whole chicken for a short time in the oven (do not over-heat). Put on to a dish and pour the sauce over this and top with parsley.
Serves 4.

Variations:
Joint the chicken or cut slices of turkey into fingers and heat in the hot sauce; in this case use a little extra liquid, as some will evaporate as the chicken heats. Use half wine and half skimmed milk to make a creamier type sauce. Use all red wine or half red wine and half stock, do not blend milk with the red wine, but stir 1–2 tablespoons natural yogurt into the thickened sauce. Use dehydrated or sliced onions in place of the cocktail onions.

Veal Escalopes with Lemon

Approx. 279 calories per portion

The veal only takes 15 minutes to cook, so any vegetables you may want to serve with the meat could be cooked before, kept hot in the saucepan in which they were cooked, then quickly tossed in butter and reheated at the last moment.

1 oz. (2 tablespoons) butter
2 escalopes of veal
1 tablespoon flour
salt and pepper

2 tablespoons lemon juice
2 tablespoons sherry
good pinch sugar
4 tablespoons natural yogurt

Heat the butter gently in a frying pan. Lightly coat the veal with the flour seasoned with salt and pepper. Fry the veal for about 10 minutes, turning once. Remove from the pan and place on a serving dish. Add the lemon juice, sherry and sugar to the pan and heat for 2 minutes. Stir in the yogurt and heat *without allowing the sauce to boil*. Spoon over the veal and serve.
Serves 2.

Variation:
Pork fillet (tenderloin) (cook for about 15 minutes) or chicken breasts (cook for about 20 minutes) could be used in place of veal.

Table-top Cookery

This rather special form of cooking allows the artistic talents of the slimmer to come to the fore. Whether cooking for yourself or entertaining, it gives you the opportunity to cook at the table. All you require is a fondue set, or a table burner with a suitable size frying pan, preferably one that is attractive to put on the table and not too solid on the base.

Once you have tried this form of cooking, you will find it quite straightforward. Most of the dishes in this section are quick to cook, which is a boon when you are short of time and have to get a meal together quickly.

PIQUANT VEAL ESCALOPES (*Photograph by Tabasco Pepper Sauce*)

Piquant Veal Escalopes

Approx. 244 calories per portion

4 escalopes of veal
salt, pepper, flour
2 oz. ($\frac{1}{4}$ cup) butter
6 spring onions (scallions)
1 lemon, sliced

2 teaspoons rosemary
$\frac{1}{4}$ teaspoon Tabasco
$\frac{1}{4}$ pint ($\frac{2}{3}$ cup) Vermouth
1 tablespoon chopped parsley

Preparation
Pound the escalopes very thinly and cut each in half. Coat
lightly with seasoned flour and set aside until required.

At the table
Heat the butter until foamy, put in the meat and fry until
golden, turning once. Remove from the pan and keep hot.
Add a little more butter to the pan if necessary and fry the
chopped white part of the onions until soft. Replace the veal,
add the thinly sliced un-peeled lemon, rosemary, Tabasco and
Vermouth. Simmer for 2-3 minutes, then check the seasoning
and sprinkle with the chopped green part of the onions and
chopped parsley.
Serves 4

Escalopes with Fennel

Approx. 206 calories per portion

1$\frac{1}{2}$ oz. (3 tablespoons) butter
4 escalopes of veal
salt, pepper
6–8 spring onions (scallions),
    chopped

3–4 tablespoons chopped
    fennel leaves
lemon juice

Heat the butter in the pan until foaming. Put in the meat and
sprinkle with salt, pepper and the chopped onions. Cover and
cook for 7-8 minutes. Sprinkle with the fennel and add a good
squeeze of lemon juice.
Serve the escalopes and spoon the juices left in the pan on top.
A green salad is the best accompaniment.
Serves 4

White Fish Fondue

Approx. 200 calories per portion

In this recipe the fish is cooked in stock instead of oil.
Fillets of white fish – sole, plaice, cod, fresh haddock etc. are all suitable.

Allow about 6 oz. fish per person

Bouillon

fish trimmings and bones	1 bay leaf
1 onion, peeled and chopped	few sprigs parsley
1–2 sticks celery, chopped	$\frac{1}{2}$ pint ($1\frac{1}{4}$ cups) dry white wine
1 carrot, peeled and chopped	1–2 teaspoons soy sauce

Preparation

Prepare the fish and cut into $1\frac{1}{2}$-2 inch squares.
Put fish trimmings and bones into a saucepan, add the vegetables, bay leaf and parsley and just enough water to cover. Bring to boiling point then skim well. Cover, reduce the heat and simmer for 30 minutes. Strain and season to taste.

At the table

Pour the fish stock into the fondue pan, add the wine and soy sauce and heat to boiling point.
Your guests can now spear the pieces of fish and put them into the boiling stock. They will cook very quickly.
Have some small dishes of soy sauce and chopped cucumber as accompaniments.

Steak au Poivre

Approx. 365 calories per portion

2 entrecôte or rump steaks,
about ¾ inch thick
1 tablespoon black
peppercorns

½ teaspoon seasoned salt
1 teaspoon seasoned pepper
1½ oz. (3 tablespoons) butter
lemon juice

Preparation

Prepare the steaks at least 2 hours before you are ready to cook them. Crush the peppercorns with a rolling pin, beat the steaks lightly, then roll in the peppercorns and press them in well. Sprinkle with the seasoned salt and pepper and leave to marinate.

In the picture, you will see the steak is served with grilled tomatoes. If you wish to do this, it would be best to grill the tomatoes just before your guests arrive, then they can be put into the pan with the steaks to reheat at the last minute.

At the table

Heat 1 oz. (2 tablespoons) butter in the pan, put in the steaks and cook for 3–4 minutes on each side depending whether your guests like them rare or medium. Put on to the serving plates, add an extra tablespoon butter to the pan and swirl it around until it just begins to colour. Add a squeeze of lemon juice and pour over the steaks.

Serves 2.

STEAK AU POIVRE (*Photograph by Lawry's Foods Inc.*)

Chicken with Almonds

Approx. 465 calories per portion

1 spring chicken, jointed
1 teaspoon salt
¼ teaspoon black pepper
2 tablespoons flour

1½ oz. (3 tablespoons) butter
¼ teaspoon marjoram
1 oz. (¼ cup) almonds

Preparation
Coat the chicken pieces with seasoned flour.

At the table
Heat the butter in the chafing dish. Put in the chicken and brown on both sides.
Add the marjoram and nuts, cover, and cook over low heat until the chicken is tender. This will take about 15-20 minutes.
A green salad is a good accompaniment.
Serves 2

Chicken with Herbs

Approx. 385 calories per portion

1 spring chicken
1 oz. (2 tablespoons) butter
2 teaspoons flour
salt, pepper
6 tablespoons white wine
¼ teaspoon thyme

¼ teaspoon rosemary
1 tablespoon finely chopped
  parsley
1 tablespoon finely chopped
  chives

Preparation
Joint the chicken and dry thoroughly.

At the table
Heat the butter in the pan, put in the chicken joints and brown all over. Sprinkle with the flour and add a little salt and pepper. Add the wine and herbs. Turn the chicken over once or twice and cook over low heat until the chicken is tender, about 15-20 minutes. Correct the seasoning before serving.
Serves 2

Beef Stroganoff

Approx. 384 calories per portion

This is an excellent dish for entertaining but it needs fairly long cooking, so have it prepared and simmering on the table when your guests arrive. The stroganoff is generally served with noodles or rice so have this prepared and kept hot or serve with a salad.

1 lb. good quality stewing
   beef
2 oz. ($\frac{1}{4}$ cup) butter
2 small onions, peeled and
   finely chopped
$\frac{1}{4}$ lb. sliced mushrooms

salt, black pepper, nutmeg
$\frac{1}{2}$ teaspoon basil
$\frac{1}{4}$ pint ($\frac{2}{3}$ cup) beef stock
$\frac{1}{2}$ pint ($1\frac{1}{4}$ cups) natural yogurt
2 tablespoons finely chopped
   parsley or chives

Cut the meat into thin slices and then into strips. Heat the butter in the pan, add the onions and sauté until transparent. Add the meat and brown over fairly high heat. Reduce the heat and add the mushrooms, salt, pepper, pinch of nutmeg, basil and stock. Bring to the boil, then cover and simmer for about 45 minutes. Add the yogurt, check the seasoning and reheat but do not allow the mixture to boil at this stage. Sprinkle with parsley or chives.
Serves 4

Pork with Spicy Orange Sauce

Approx. 395 calories per portion

1¼ lb. pork fillet (tenderloin)
salt, pepper, flour
1 oz. (2 tablespoons) butter
1 small onion, peeled and
  chopped
1 green pepper, blanched,
  seeded and cut into strips

3 oranges
grated rind of ½ orange
1 tablespoon Worcestershire
  sauce
¼ pint (⅔ cup) stock

Preparation

Trim the meat and cut into 1 inch cubes. Coat with seasoned flour.
Peel one of the oranges, remove all the white pith and cut into segments.

At the table

Heat the butter in the pan, add the onion and green pepper and sauté for 3 minutes. Add the meat and cook for 5 minutes, turning frequently. Add the juice of 2 oranges and ½ teaspoon grated orange rind then add Worcestershire sauce and stock. Bring to boiling point and simmer for 10 minutes, stirring occasionally.
Check the seasoning and add the orange segments just before serving.
A green salad is a good accompaniment.
Serves 4

Desserts

Contrary to the thoughts of many would-be slimmers, puddings can be included in a diet, as long as they are the right type and not the 'apple pie with double portion of cream' variety.

Fruit can form the base of many low-calorie desserts, making a refreshing, light finish to a meal. Fruits, such as apples, pears and oranges, can be baked in the oven with a little fruit juice and artificial sweetener to taste, and then topped with low-fat natural yogurt before serving. There are recipes for Baked Apples and Baked Oranges (page 76), and a delicious recipe for Apple Water Ice (page 75).

A small quantity of cream is included in some of the recipes, to fit in with the portion calorie count, but don't be tempted to serve it as an extra accompaniment. This will quickly transform a low-calorie pudding into a high-calorie one!

Apple Water Ice

Approx. 118 calories per portion

1 lb. cooking apples
1 lemon
½ pint (1¼ cups) water
4 oz. (½ cup) sugar

2 teaspoons powdered gelatine
colouring
1 egg white
Garnish:
mint leaves

Wash and chop the apples, do not remove peel or cores, as these give flavour. Put into a saucepan with the thinly pared lemon rind, water and sugar. Simmer until the apples are very soft. Sieve the mixture, return to the pan to keep warm. Soften the gelatine in the cold lemon juice, add to the warm apple mixture, and stir until dissolved. Taste, and add extra sugar as desired, or if the apples are rather sweet add a little more lemon juice. Tint the juice a delicate shade of green or pink. Cool, and then freeze. Pour into freezing trays or a deeper utensil. Freeze on the normal setting in the refrigerator or home freezer. Leave until lightly frosted. Remove and blend with the stiffly beaten egg white. Return to the freezing compartment or freezer and continue freezing. Serve in glasses, or pile into fresh peach halves, and decorate with mint leaves. The combination of the sharp apple mixture and the sweet peach is delicious.
Serves 6, or 8 when served with other ingredients, such as peaches.

Variations:
Use other fruit in place of apples. Plums, damsons, rhubarb, gooseberries, etc., should be cooked. Raspberries, strawberries and other soft fruits should be used raw and blended with the syrup, made by heating the water, sugar and lemon rind. Two fruits can also be blended together.

To prepare in advance:
Water ices, like ice creams, are an excellent choice when planning ahead. Bring out of the freezing compartment or freezer a little while before serving. Pile into the peach halves then return to the freezer for a very short time, otherwise the peaches become too hard.

Baked Apples

Approx. 97 calories per portion

4 medium-sized to large cooking apples | approximately 4 tablespoons brown or white sugar

Core the apples; do this either with an apple corer or a pointed knife. In order to prevent the skin bursting during cooking make a light slit round the centre of the apples. Put the apples into an oven-proof dish, fill the centres with sugar. Bake for approximately 1 hour in the centre of a moderate oven, 350–375°F, Mark 4–5, or allow 15 minutes longer in a very moderate oven, 325°F, Mark 3. The skin may be left on the apples. Serve with natural yogurt.
Serves 4

Variation:
Baked Apples with Orange Filling: Ingredients as for baked apples minus the sugar, plus 2–3 tablespoons of orange marmalade, the finely grated rind of 1–2 oranges and approximately 2 tablespoons orange juice. Blend the marmalade, grated rind and juice and put into the apples before cooking.
While the apples are cooking, cut neat pieces of orange segments. Remove the apples from the oven a few minutes before serving, spoon the orange segments on top, return to the oven to heat; or omit orange pieces and decorate with strips of rind.

Baked Oranges

Approx. 176 calories per portion

4 large oranges | 2 oz. ($\frac{1}{3}$ cup) brown sugar
1 oz. (2 tablespoons) butter | 3 tablespoons rum

Try and choose the seedless variety of orange. Cut away the peel and also the outer pith. Cut the oranges across the centre and put into a lightly buttered dish, with the cut sides uppermost. Top with brown sugar, rum and rest of the butter. Bake for 20–25 minutes in a moderate oven, 350–375°F, Mark 4–5.
Serves 4.

BAKED APPLES WITH ORANGE FILLING

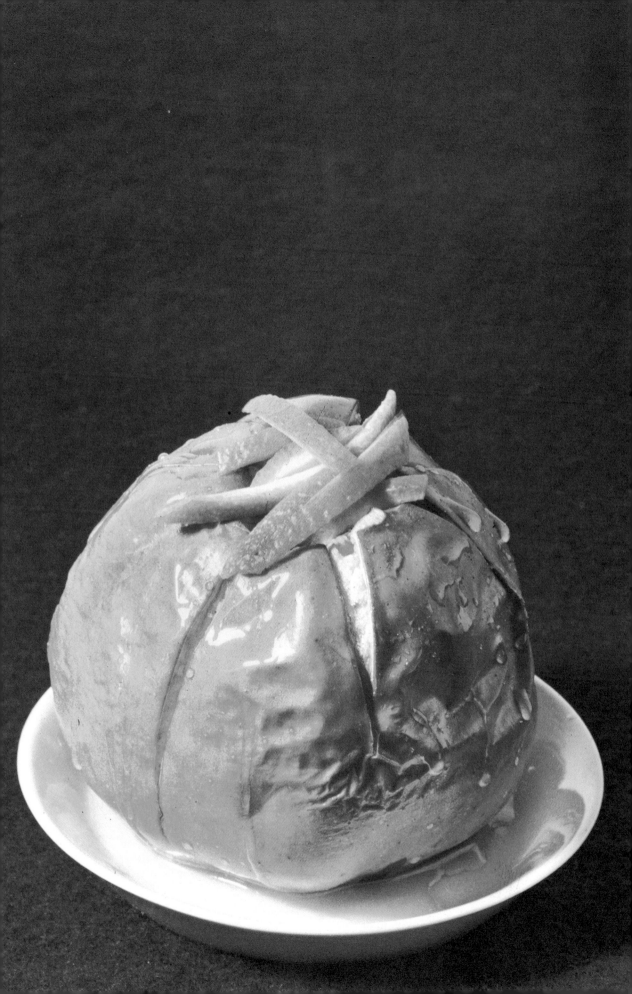

Lemon Soufflé

Approx. 143 calories per portion

finely grated rind of 2 lemons
4 tablespoons lemon juice
3 eggs
4 oz. (½ cup) castor
  (superfine) sugar

¾ tablespoon powdered gelatine
4 tablespoons water
½ pint (1¼ cups) natural yogurt
Decoration:
small ratafia biscuits (cookies)

Put the lemon rind, juice, egg yolks and sugar into a basin over a pan of very hot water. Whisk until thick and creamy. Soften the gelatine in the cold water, and add to the egg yolk mixture, stirring over the heat until the gelatine has dissolved. Cool and allow to stiffen slightly.
Fold the yogurt into the jellied mixture. Whisk the egg whites until stiff, but not too dry, fold into the mixture. Spoon into the prepared soufflé dish, see below. Allow to set and remove the paper slowly and carefully. Press some finely crushed ratafia biscuits (cookies) on to the sides of the soufflé and decorate the top with ratafias.
Serves 5–6.

To prepare a soufflé dish:
Cut a band of greaseproof (waxed) paper three times the depth of the dish. Fold to give a double thickness, and brush the part that will stand above the dish with a very light coating of melted butter. Tie or pin the band of paper very securely round the outside of the soufflé dish.

Variations:
Use orange rind and juice instead of lemon rind and juice.
Use 6 tablespoons (½ cup) water plus 2 tablespoons crème de menthe or other liqueur in the recipe above, omitting the lemon rind and juice.
Use ¼ pint (⅔ cup) fruit purée instead of the lemon juice, and reduce the water to 2 tablespoons. Omit the lemon rind.
Omit the lemon rind and juice and add 3 oz. plain chocolate to the egg yolks, etc.

Fruit Chiffon

Approx. 83 calories per portion

2 teaspoons gelatine
2 tablespoons lemon juice
½ pint (1¼ cups) sweetened
   thick fruit purée

¼ pint (⅔ cup) natural yogurt
2 egg whites
1 oz. (2 tablespoons) sugar

Soften the gelatine in the cold lemon juice then stand over hot water until dissolved. Stir into the fruit purée. Leave until lightly set then fold in the natural yogurt. Whisk the egg whites until very stiff, whisk in the sugar, then fold this meringue mixture into the fruit, etc. Spoon into the glasses.
Serves 4–5.

Banana Cream Syllabub

Approx. 75 calories per portion

3 ripe firm bananas
2 tablespoons lemon juice
2 tablespoons white wine

1 oz. (2 tablespoons) sugar
½ pint (1¼ cups) natural yogurt

Peel the bananas and mash with the lemon juice, wine and sugar. Fold the yogurt into the banana mixture. Spoon into serving dishes and chill before serving.
Serves 6

Gooseberry Sparkle

Approx. 130 calories per portion

1 packet lime or other flavoured
  jelly
1 medium can gooseberries

Decoration:
whipped cream
chopped glacé cherries
chopped crystallized ginger

Read the instructions on the packet for the exact amount of
water or liquid required; this varies slightly according to
different makes. Strain off the syrup from the can of fruit and
dilute with water to make up to the quantity given on the
packet less about 1 tablespoon. This is because the fruit is
moist and will dilute the strength of the jelly.
Dissolve the jelly according to the instructions. Pour a little
into a rinsed mould. Allow this to become nearly set and
arrange the first layer of fruit on top. It is easier to do this
if you dip the fruit in liquid jelly. When set pour over a little
more jelly and continue filling the mould like this to give an
interesting design. Allow to set and turn out. Decorate with
a little whipped cream, chopped glacé cherries and chopped
crystallized ginger.
Serves 4.

Variations:
Use other flavoured jellies and fruits in the same way.
Harlequin Jelly: Omit the fruit and use water plus a little
fresh orange or lemon juice to give the quantity recommended
on the packet. When the jelly is cold and just beginning to
stiffen add the following: 3 tablespoons of diced glacé
cherries, 2 tablespoons raisins or sultanas, 2 tablespoons
quartered marshmallows and 2 tablespoons coarsely chopped
walnuts. Stir into the jelly and put into a mould, rinsed in
cold water, allow to set.
Milk Jelly: Take any fruit flavoured jelly and dissolve in
$\frac{1}{4}$ pint ($\frac{2}{3}$ cup) very hot water. When this is cold add $\frac{3}{4}$ pint
(2 cups) cold skimmed milk. Allow to set.

GOOSEBERRY SPARKLE *(Photograph by Cadbury Schweppes Food Advisory
Service, Bournville, Birmingham, England)*

Orange and Pear Caprice

Approx. 144 calories per portion

3 oz. ($\frac{3}{8}$ cup) sugar
$\frac{1}{4}$ pint ($\frac{2}{3}$ cup) water
1 x 6 fl. oz. can concentrated
    frozen orange juice, thawed.

1 egg white
2 oranges
1 pear
lemon juice

Put the sugar and water into a saucepan and heat slowly until the sugar has dissolved. Remove from the heat and allow to cool. Stir in the orange juice (do not dilute this) and mix well. Turn into a small container and freeze in the ice-making compartment of the refrigerator for about 2 hours, or until it is barely firm.
Remove from the refrigerator, turn into a bowl and mash with a fork so that no large lumps remain. Stiffly whisk the egg white in a separate bowl and fold into the orange mixture. Spoon back into the container and return to the refigerator. Freeze until firm; this will take about 6 hours.
Remove the peel from the oranges, using a sharp knife, and divide into segments, leaving the orange segments free from skin. Peel, core and slice the pear and sprinkle with lemon juice to preserve the colour.
Scoop the water ice into glasses and decorate with the orange and pear segments.
Serves 4.

Note : If you are in a hurry use commercially-made water ice – either orange or tangerine flavour.

Drinks, Sauces and Extras

This section contains a lot of edible and drinkable extras for slimmers; a selection of hot and cold drinks, to drink with and between meals, and a number of sauces to serve with low-calorie meat and fish dishes. There is a recipe for Muesli (page 91), which is ideal as a complete low-calorie breakfast, mixed with skimmed milk.

Hollandaise Sauce

Approx. 120 calories per portion

3 egg yolks
salt
pepper

cayenne pepper
2 tablespoons lemon juice*
3 oz. ($\frac{3}{8}$ cup) butter

*Or use white wine vinegar.

Put the egg yolks, seasoning and lemon juice into a basin over a pan of hot water or into the top of a double saucepan. Make sure the basin or alternative utensil is sufficiently large to be able to whisk well; a very narrow container hampers movement. Beat with a hand or electric whisk until the mixture is light and fluffy.

If using an electric whisk check that the egg mixture is thickening well. To do this remove from the heat, if the eggs remain thick all is well. Sometimes one can whisk so vigorously that the mixture appears to thicken, then 'flops', as it has just been aerated, not cooked as it should be. When the eggs are thick, add a small piece of butter and whisk hard until well blended. Continue like this until all the butter is incorporated. Serve hot or cold over vegetables or with fish. This is an excellent sauce for cauliflower, broccoli or asparagus.

All recipes based on this serve 6–7.

Devilled Sauce

Approx. 74 calories per portion

3 large onions
3 tablespoons olive oil
1–2 tablespoons Worcestershire
   sauce
up to 1 teaspoon Tabasco or chilli
   sauce

shake cayenne pepper
pinch curry powder
good pinch salt
$\frac{1}{4}$ pint ($\frac{2}{3}$ cup) red wine
$\frac{1}{4}$ pint ($\frac{2}{3}$ cup) beef stock

Chop or grate the onions very finely, then mix with the oil
and Worcestershire and Tabasco or chilli sauce. Add the
pepper, curry powder and salt. Brush the meat with this
mixture just before cooking, then baste with the mixture
during cooking. Add the wine and stock towards the end of
the cooking time and heat to make a sauce.
Serves 6.

Variations:
To thicken the sauce: Either blend 2 tablespoons tomato
ketchup with the wine and stock, this thickens slightly as
well as giving extra flavour, or blend 1 tablespoon cornflour
(cornstarch) with the wine and stock, and heat until
thickened; then add the onion mixture.
To serve with fish: Use 1 onion only and add the grated
rind and juice of 1–2 lemons to the oil. Use all white wine, or
half white wine and half water or fish stock. The sauce can
be thickened with tomato ketchup, as suggested in the
variation above, or with cornflour (cornstarch).
To serve with poultry: Add 1–2 cloves crushed garlic to the
onions – these can be used with meat also.
Be rather more sparing with the sauces and add finely chopped
fresh thyme towards the end of the cooking period.

Basic Mayonnaise Sauce

Approx. 175 calories per portion

2 egg yolks
½ teaspoon French mustard
½ teaspoon each of sugar and
   salt
pinch of white pepper

small pinch of cayenne pepper
few drops lemon juice
½ pint (1¼ cups) corn oil
2–3 tablespoons white wine
   vinegar

Put the yolks into a small bowl, add seasonings and lemon juice and work together for a few minutes using a wooden spoon. Add 2 tablespoons oil 2-3 drops at a time. The mixture should now be thick. Dilute with 2 teaspoons vinegar, then continue to add the oil carefully at first, then more quickly as the sauce thickens. Add a little more vinegar from time to time. When completed, the sauce should be thick enough to keep its shape. Adjust the seasoning. Finally, add 1 tablespoon boiling water.
Serves 6–8.

Tartare Sauce Add 4 tablespoons chopped capers, 2 tablespoons chopped gherkins and 1 tablespoon chopped parsley to the basic mayonnaise.

Andalouse Sauce Add 4 tablespoons tomato paste and 4 tablespoons finely chopped pimiento to the basic sauce.

Curry Sauce Add curry paste to taste.

Remoulade Sauce Add 2 tablespoons finely chopped dill pickle or gherkin, 2 teaspoons finely chopped capers, 1 teaspoon French mustard, 2 teaspoons finely chopped parsley, a dash of Tabasco and 2 tablespoons natural yogurt to the basic mayonnaise.

Note: The above are all accompanying sauces which slimmers can afford to eat only in small quantities. For this reason, mayonnaise has not been used as a recipe ingredient within the book.

Fruit Punch

Approx. 55 calories per glass

4 apples
4 tablespoons honey
6 cloves
2 sticks cinnamon
1 pint (2½ cups) water
1 pint (2½ cups) pineapple juice

1 pint (2½ cups) orange juice
1 pint (2½ cups) soda water
4 oz. seedless grapes
ice cubes
mint sprigs

Peel and slice the apples. Put them in a saucepan with the honey, spices and water and simmer until pulpy. Strain and chill.

Mix the apple liquid with the fruit juices in a large bowl or jug. Pour in the soda water.

Add the grapes and ice cubes and garnish with mint sprigs. **Serves 12–14.**

Summer Tea

Approx. 30 calories per glass

2 pints (5 cups) fragrant China tea
2 pints (5 cups) orange juice
1 pint (2½ cups) apple juice
1 pint (2½ cups) white grape juice
½ tablespoon Angostura bitters

large block of ice
mint sprigs, berries and orange
  slices to garnish
soda water

Mix tea, fruit juices and Angostura bitters in a large punch bowl. Add the ice.

Garnish with mint sprigs, berries and orange slices.

Serve in tall glasses, with soda added to taste. **Serves about 20.**

Peppermint Tea

Approx. 25 calories per glass

2½ teaspoons peppermint tea
  leaves
1 pint (2½ cups) water

2 tablespoons honey
1 cup crushed ice

Boil water and brew tea. Allow to stand for about 10 minutes, then pour water off leaves.
Add honey and allow to cool. Add crushed ice before serving.
Serves 4.

Note: peppermint tea is available in some continental delicatessen, and in health food stores.

Fruit Froth

Approx. 120 calories per glass

6 fl. oz. (¾ cup) black cherry
  juice
6 fl. oz. (¾ cup) pineapple juice
2 fl. oz. (¼ cup) lemon juice

1 egg white
1 cup crushed ice
whole stewed black cherries to
  decorate

Shake juices and egg white well with ice. Strain into two tall glasses. Decorate with cherries.
Serves 2.

Simple Apple Muesli

Approx. 202 calories per portion

2 tablespoons rolled oats
1 tablespoon lemon juice
¾ pint (2 cups) skimmed milk
2 tablespoons honey

1 large apple
1 tablespoon grated nuts
1 tablespoon sultanas (golden
   raisins)

The prepared, so-called 'quick' oats need not be soaked;
otherwise, soak the oats or oatmeal for about 12 hours
(overnight), in 3 tablespoons water.
Mix the lemon juice with the milk and honey and pour over
the oats. Grate the apple into the mixture and stir in with the
nuts and sultanas (raisins). Serve at once, as the apple
discolours and the oats become very soft.
Serves 2.

Variation:
Other soft, fresh fruits may be added, such as bananas or
strawberries. Try low fat natural yogurt in place of milk.

Index

Figures in italics refer to illustrations

Apple:
    Apple muesli, simple 91
    Apple water ice 75
    Baked apples 76, *77*
Artichokes vinaigrette 24, *25*
Asparagus parmesan 24
Aubergines gratinées 26
Avocado and walnut salad 28, *29*

Baked apples 76, *77*
Baked oranges 76
Banana cream syllabub 79
Beans:
    Beans niçoise 27
    Fried beans 36, *37*
Beef:
    Beef stroganoff 71
    Braised beef Neapolitan 46
    Goulash of gulyas (Hungarian paprika stew) 54
    Simple pot-au-feu 50
    Steak au poivre 68, *69*
Braised beef Neapolitan 46

Calculating calories 8
Calorie chart 12
Chaudfroid of fish 40
Chicken:
    Chicken noodle soup 22
    Chicken with almonds 70
    Chicken with herbs 70
    Coq au vin 62
    Devilled chicken *4*, 59
    Dry chicken curry with yellow rice 44, *45*
    Oriental chicken 47
    Spatchcock of chicken 43
    Sweet and sour chicken salad 48, *49*
Chinese-style vegetable soup *17*, 18
Coleslaw 35
Coq au vin 62
Courgettes à la provençale 31

Devilled chicken *4*, 59
Devilled sauce 86
Drinks:
    Fruit froth 90
    Fruit punch 88, *89*
    Peppermint tea 90
    Summer tea 88
Dry chicken curry with yellow rice 44, *45*

Escalopes, piquant veal *65*, 66
Escalopes with fennel 66
Escalopes of veal with lemon *13*, 63

Fish:
    Chaudfroid of fish 40
    Haddock soufflé 41
    Savoury grilled (broiled) turbot 39
    Spiced fish soup 23
    Tuna salad 35
    White fish fondue 67
Fried beans 36, *37*
Frosted tomato cocktail 20, *21*
Fruit chiffon 79
Fruit froth 90
Fruit punch 88, *89*

Gooseberry sparkle 80, *81*
Goulash of gulyas (Hungarian paprika stew) 54
Grapefruit jellied salad 34

Haddock soufflé 41
Hare in Madeira sauce 52, *53*
Hollandaise sauce 84, *85*
Hungarian paprika stew (Goulash of gulyas) 54

Lamb:
    Lamb shish-kebabs with herbed sauce 60, *61*
    Lemon and ginger chops 56, *57*
    Tajine tfaia (Moroccan lamb dish) 51
Lemon:
    Lemon and ginger chops 56, *57*
    Lemon soufflé 78
Liver:
    Liver ragoût 59

Mayonnaise sauce, basic 87
Moroccan lamb dish (Tajine tfaia) 51
Muesli, simple apple 91

Onion and pepper soup 19
Orange:
    Baked oranges 76
    Orange and pear caprice 82
Oriental chicken 47

Peppermint tea 90
Piquant veal escalopes *65*, 66
Pork:
    Pork with spicy orange sauce 72, *73*
    Somerset pork *9*, 58
Pot-au-feu, simple 50

Ratatouille 32, *33*
Rice:
    Rice and lemon soup 18
    Yellow rice 44

Salads:
    Coleslaw 35
    Grapefruit jellied salad 34
    Savoury tongue salad 35
    Sweet and sour chicken salad 48, *49*
    Tuna salad 35
    Walnut and avocado salad 28, *29*
Sauces:
    Devilled sauce 86
    Herbed sauce 60
    Hollandaise sauce 84, *85*
    Mayonnaise sauce, basic 87
Savoury grilled (broiled) turbot 39
Savoury tongue salad 35
Simple apple muesli 91
Simple pot-au-feu 50
Slimming tips 11
Somerset pork *9*, 58
Soufflé, lemon 78
Soups:
    Chicken noodle soup 22
    Chinese-style vegetable soup *17*, 18
    Onion and pepper soup 19
    Rice and lemon soup 18
    Spiced fish soup 23
Spatchcock of chicken 43
Spiced fish soup 23
Steak au poivre 68, *69*
Stroganoff, beef 71
Summer tea 88
Sweet and sour chicken salad 48, *49*
Syllabub, banana cream 79

Tajine tfaia (Moroccan lamb dish) 51
Tomatoes:
    Frosted tomato cocktail 20, *21*
Tongue salad 35
Tuna salad 35
Turbot, savoury grilled (broiled) 39

Veal:
    Escalopes with fennel 66
    Piquant veal escalopes *65*, 66
    Veal escalopes with lemon *13*, 63
    Veal fricassée 43
    Wiener schnitzel 55
Vegetable soup, Chinese-style *17*, 18

Walnut and avocado salad 28, *29*
Weight charts 10
White fish fondue 67
Wiener schnitzel 55

The publishers wish to thank the following for their contribution to the book:

John Lee
Norman Nicholls
Syndication International
Bryce Attwell
New Idea magazine
Phoebe's Health Food Shop, Sydney and Mervyn Clark
Casa Pupo Shop, David Jones, Sydney
Crown Corning Pty, Ltd
Incorporated Agencies Pty. Ltd, Sydney
Opus Design Shop, Sydney
Phil Dunn by courtesy of The Potters Gallery, Sydney
Rosenthall Studio-Line, Sydney
The Bay Tree Pty. Ltd, Sydney
Vasa Agencies Pty. Ltd, Sydney